CHARLES BORROMEO

PRINCE OF PASTORS

by
J.B.Midgley

All booklets are published thanks to the generous support of the members of the Catholic Truth Society

CATHOLIC TRUTH SOCIETY
PUBLISHERS TO THE HOLY SEE

CONTENTS

INTRODUCTION

Whenever the Church encounters periodic difficulties, God raises up holy men and women to restore confidence and give guidance to his People. Among them are successors to the Apostles, the Shepherds to whom Christ entrusts the care of His Flock. A shining example is Charles Borromeo, the great Catholic reformer of the sixteenth century. A bishop within twelve months of his ordination to the priesthood, the Cardinal-Archbishop of Milan understood that the pastoral episcopate was central to the renewal of Faith, and this "Prince of Pastors" became the Council of Trent's model bishop who, like the Good Shepherd, cherished the dignity of the individual person, and cared for those in physical or spiritual need.

He was motivated by zeal for God's glory, his eyes ever on the central figure of Christ who brings all things into being, and shares human nature to bring His brothers and sisters to their inheritance in the Kingdom of the Father. He attached the greatest importance to the education and continued development of priests who celebrate the Sacrifice of the Mass which is at the heart of Catholic life, who preach the Gospel, administer the Sacraments as channels of sanctifying grace, and who teach God's People how to love and praise Him. In his new and reformed seminaries, therefore, he appointed devoted Rectors who were faithful to the teachings of the Church, and unequivocally loyal to the successor of St Peter.

The Collect of the Mass for Saint Charles Borromeo's Feast identifies his outstanding virtues, his wisdom, love, and care for God's People, and reminds us of the relevance of his intercession throughout time, not least in our own. "Lord, keep your Church under the continual protection of your holy Bishop and Confessor Charles. Let the intercession of one so renowned for the watchful care of his flock, kindle in us an ever burning love of You."

It was in his honour that Pope John XXIII chose to open the Second Vatican Council in 1962 on 4th November, Charles Borromeo's feast day.

Downham Market, Solemnity of the Assumption of the Most Blessed Virgin Mary, 2005

The Formative Years

The Borromeo family were landowners from Tuscany who moved to Lombardy and won wealth and status in Milan. No sooner had they arrived than they built themselves an imposing palace in the city centre opposite the church of Santa Maria de Podone. In the fifteenth century, Filippo Visconti, third Duke of Milan, gave the tenancy of the Castle of Arona, near Lake Maggiore and fourteen miles from Milan, to Vitaliano Borromeo with control of the surrounding country estates, and ennobled him with the title of Count.

By the time Charles Borromeo's father Count Gilberto succeeded to the title, life was dangerous and possessions were in hazard because repeated invasions by Spanish and French armed forces, and the accession of the Holy Roman Emperor Charles V in 1520 had deprived Italy of independence. Thanks to considerable ingenuity and influential contacts, Gilberto managed to keep the palace in Milan, the territories by Lake Maggiore, and retain command of the garrison in the Castle of Arona. By 1530, he felt he could safely contemplate marriage, and chose as his bride Margaret Medici. She was a remarkably gentle and virtuous girl who proved a wonderful wife and mother universally loved by her household, tenants, and the poor and sick in Arona and Milan whom she helped not only with alms, but by her active involvement in alleviating their situation. One of her brothers was Cardinal Giovanni Angelo Medici, who would become Pope Pius IV.

A religious upbringing

Gilberto could be an impatient and demanding master, husband and parent, but he was always scrupulously fair, and there was no doubting his piety. He recited the Divine Office every day, and went to Communion twice a week which was rare in those days, and fasted frequently. He had a great devotion to the Blessed Sacrament which he transmitted to his family, and when the bell rang in the Chapel everyone in the castle, soldiers, workers, children, had to stop everything and rush to be present at the moment of Consecration during the Mass. He and Margaret brought up their children to know the importance of prayer as a natural part of life, and that it accompanied almsgiving to assist those in need. Every day, before his own meal, Gilberto distributed food and money to villagers, peasants and travellers who stood at the castle gates. His pension from the emperor and the rents from the Arona estates gave him a reasonable income, but the expense of running the garrison, the castle, and the palace in Milan, caused some financial problems. Nevertheless, his confidence in Divine Providence and his generosity remained steadfast.

Limitations and piety

Gilberto and Margaret had four daughters and two sons. Charles, the second boy, was born on October 2nd 1538 in Arona Castle, and his father was so pleased that he commissioned a portrait of the baby, unusual in that infants were considered barely distinguishable from one another. In this case, however, the wide, dark eyes are intent, the face already serious, and the tiny hands determined. The nurse looks as if she might have trouble restraining her eager handful. The first son, Frederick, grew to be handsome, good at games and riding, but was not particularly interested in his studies. Charles was less immediately attractive, had inherited Gilberto's pronounced aquiline nose, and by nature was serious and retiring, no doubt because he was embarrassed by an early speech impediment which made him stammer and then explode with a rush of words which were difficult to understand. This also explains the special love and care with which his mother watched over him.

He loved horses who served him well on his many travels often over difficult terrain throughout his life, had a sensitive appreciation of music, and became an accomplished performer on the lute and cello. Scholarship did not come easily to him, though he more than compensated for any lack of aptitude by a capacity for hard work and attention to detail. It was taken for granted that, as a second son, he was destined for a career in the Church and, indeed, from his earliest years he used to erect altars and conduct child-like services. As he matured, however, it was his genuine piety, devotion to the Blessed Sacrament, the liturgy, and the Divine Office which pointed to his high calling.

He was only nine when his beloved mother died and one can only guess at his heart-break. His father re-married on two occasions and, fortunately, relationships with the step-mothers were comfortingly close, in the latter case even after Gilberto's death. Three years later, he received the tonsure, the minor order which technically made him a cleric entitled to receive ecclesiastic benefices without the inconvenience of duties. His uncle, Julius Caesar Borromeo, immediately resigned as titular abbot of the Abbey of Arona dedicated to Saint Gratian and Saint Felinus, and nominated Charles to take his place.

The annual income of about £13,000 from this tenth century Benedictine foundation had long provided an enviable income for clerics in the Medici family, but for a century it had suffered from titular abbots and, like many religious houses, had lost its original fervour. Charles decided that the revenues should be used to assist the poor and that only a modest amount would be retained by his father to assist with his education to serve the Church. He also allowed Gilberto to borrow funds to meet some pressing demands, but kept an accurate account to make sure that all loans were repaid. In an age when decadence and corruption were the norm, such integrity is the more admirable.

For the next two years Charles was educated in Milan under the tuition of the holy and learned Ambrosian Rector Joseph Perla who was an authority on the Gaulish ancestry of the Lombards. It seems Gilberto kept his son on a minimum allowance, for on December 7th 1551, the young student wrote to him in Latin, "Could I forget you? The stars would fall, the sun be darkened, the heavens stricken still before that… I will not tell you much about my work, except that I devote myself to the humanities but books are needed. So I beg and pray you earnestly to buy me Pliny, Aristotle's 'de Animalibus', and Sallust which cost a hundred sesterces." It was the first of a number of pleas for money, the shortage of which would be a problem throughout his student life.

University years

The University of Pavia, about twenty-five miles south of Milan, was one of nine founded in Italy by Charlemagne's grandson, the emperor Lothair, and its first principal in 825 was the learned Dougal from Ireland. It fell into decay in the middle ages but was revived in 1361 by Bernabo and Galeazzo Visconti who established chairs of jurisprudence and opened a library for the benefit of students of all disciplines. Charles was fourteen when he enrolled to read Civil and Canon Law and, by this time, the university was recovering its former prestige and was full of students from all over Europe.

He commenced studies on November 2nd 1552, and his principal tutor was Francesco Alciato. For the next six years, the reserved boy developed the qualities essential to his future greatness. His close friend and biographer Father Bascape wrote, "His mental qualities did not develop quickly enough for him to make any remarkable progress", but his dedication and thorough industry ensured progress, and his conduct was a model for Renaissance students more inclined to having a good time in all sorts of ways. He was unaffected by the temptations of life in the city with its relaxed attitudes to morality, and avoided distractions that would have interfered with his prayer-life. He wrote to his uncle, the Cardinal Medici, "I shall force myself to do you credit."

As a student of noble birth, he was expected to maintain an appropriate household and, though unpretentious himself, he was conscious of a responsibility to preserve the family's dignity. Occasionally he had to use some of the revenue from the abbacy, but never for his own benefit. Once, when it was bitterly cold, he wrote home asking if he could have a cloak of the type most students wore, offering to buy it in Pavia where it would be cheaper, and then saying he would do without and keep to clerical attire. In 1553, he wrote again to his father, still distributing alms with boundless generosity, to say that he could not accept an invitation to visit his uncle in the Cardinal's splendid Marignano palace in Milan because he had "no stockings, no shoes, no cap, no doublet. I also need boots, spurs and hat." Rather unfeelingly, Gilberto suggested that he should apply for one of the charitable allowances for destitute students.

Count Gilberto was taken ill in July 1558. Charles rode posthaste to Arona where his father died in early August. Although he was not the eldest son, the family wanted him to take over management of domestic affairs since Frederick was none too reliable, and what he had to do was more complicated and took much longer than it takes to tell. He arranged the funeral and burial in Santa Maria delle Grazie in Milan, settled the estate, and made provision for his step-mother and his sisters with sensitivity and tact, especially in the case of the continued possession of the Castle of Arona.

He decided this was the time to restore monastic discipline in his Abbey much to the initial disgruntlement of the community, but eventually with the success which attended his life-long preference for example and guidance rather than fruitless confrontation. When he returned to Pavia, the worries and troubles he had shouldered brought on something of a breakdown and a hacking cough which remained with him for many years till he cured it by rigorous fasting which gave rise to the Milanese description of starvation as "St Charles' Remedy!"

A Doctor in Law

Despite these interruptions, his hard work ensured the successful completion of his studies and, though still only twenty-one, he was awarded his Doctorate in Civil and Canon Law in 1559. Not surprisingly, Charles was lean and lanky, but a severe appearance did not hide a keen sense of humour and warmth, so that he was popular with his fellow students, always the harshest critics, who admired his calm certainty and efficiency. When the scholastic year ended in July they thronged University Hall to celebrate with the Borromeo family and friends. As Francesco Alciato rose to speak the panegyric on his favourite pupil, the sun suddenly burst through hitherto gloomy skies, and the skilled orator took the opportunity to observe that such brilliance foretold the young Doctor's future greatness. Cardinal Medici was very fond and proud of his nephew, and assigned him yet another Abbey with Priory, but again Charles used the income to relieve the poor. He also began his funding of the Collegio Borromeo in Pavia which, with his Swiss College in Milan, and the College in Ascona, are illustrious examples of the seminaries he opened in response to the Council of Trent. One day, he would see to it that Alciato would be created Cardinal.

SIGNS OF REVIVAL

State of the Church in Charles's time

By the fourteenth century disorders debilitating spiritual life included the feudal inheritance of parishes by unworthy heirs, clerical immorality and concubinage, and the acquisition of lucrative ecclesiastical livings which were then left in the hands of unqualified and poorly paid substitutes. Some ecclesiastics gave priority to the preservation of the system and allowed a pursuit of political influence, social control, and wealth to deflect them from the responsibility of religious leadership. There was corruption and nepotism notoriously exemplified by the Renaissance papacy of the Borgia Alexander VI, internecine strife, the separation of piety from theology and theology from its biblical foundations, and an ignoring of the implications of scientific development and the emergence of nation-states less inclined to pay homage to Rome. The people generally remained loyal to the faith but growing dissatisfaction and anti-clericalism set the stage for reform promoted by those devoted to renewal of organisation, attitudes and values. This was the state of affairs which confronted

Charles Borromeo and others of like mind who are presented according to their year of birth. The circumstances illuminate his contribution to the Council of Trent, not just as a counter to Protestantism but as part of a single reforming impulse, and to the Church of his own and succeeding generations in God's eternal present moment.

Roots of reform

A move towards spiritual reform can be traced back to the Dutch spiritual writer, Geert de Groote, 1340-84, who had been impressed by the deeply religious Carthusian order of monks founded by St Bruno in the eleventh century. To counteract the clergy's immorality in Utrecht, he organised men and women of like mind into communities known as the Brothers and Sisters of the Common Life, and their good influence spread through Europe, particularly in the Netherlands and Germany. Their distinctive spirituality was known as *'Devotio Moderna'*, the New Devotion, which placed simple, fervent faith and the interior life in a personal relationship with Christ above theological disputation. They encouraged the spiritual life of the laity, and worked to make the scriptures and pious works in the vernacular available to them, wonderfully exemplified by Thomas a Kempis' *'Of the Imitation of Christ.'*

Erasmus

Erasmus, 1466-1536, Dutch scholar, author, and friend of Thomas More, influenced Reform by way of Christian humanism, the optimistic philosophy which sees the human being as rational, progressive, intellectual, and deserving of equality and freedom. His revised translation of the New Testament advanced the education of the laity and the cause of theology based on authentic texts. His other writings which inspired reformers of all persuasions include *"The Handbook of the Christian Soldier"*, and *"In Praise of Folly"*, in which he advocates reason, humanity, Christian charity, and a constructive, pious reform of the Church and its individual members. He maintained that Biblical studies and the teaching of the early Fathers were the foundation of Christian Doctrine, and remained a devout Catholic all his life.

John Fisher

St John Fisher, 1469-1535, was a brilliant scholar who became Chancellor of Cambridge University and Bishop of Rochester after modestly declining more prestigious diocesan appointments. Henry VIII commented that no prince ever had a more distinguished prelate. He was renowned for his preaching, education reforms, for invigorating Scholasticism with humanist ideals, and his writings in defence of Church tradition made a decisive contribution to the Council of Trent and Catholic

Reformation theology. Without much support from his fellow bishops, he voiced church opposition to Henry's divorce and his claims to supremacy over the Church in England. When Pope Paul III made him a cardinal the king remarked that he "would have no head on which to put his red hat," and he was duly executed a few days before Thomas More.

Thomas More

St Thomas More, 1478-1535, Oxford scholar and friend of Erasmus, argued as a humanist for moral and social reform through education and sacred literature. His most famous works are 'Utopia', a social satire searching for ideal government in 'Nowhere' land, and his letters written from the Tower which show a deep devotion to the sufferings of Christ. Henry had promoted him through a number of offices, culminating in the Lord Chancellorship, but his refusal to subscribe to the Act of Succession led to his imprisonment in the Tower and his beheading on July 6th 1535.

Cajetan

St Cajetan, 1480-1547, was a diocesan priest who was concerned about the devotional life of the clergy and the general state of the Church. He was a member of the 16th Century Roman Oratory of Divine Love, which had been founded in Italy under the inspiration of Catherine of

Genoa to serve charitable purposes, and which was something of a nursery of Church reformers. The exemplary community life of these diocesan priests so impressed the future Pope Paul IV that, with Cajetan, he founded the Theatines ("from the town of Chieti"), an order devoted to parish and pastoral work, the practice of poverty, evangelisation and helping the poor, known today as the Congregation Clerks Regular.

Ignatius

St Ignatius of Loyola, 1491-1556, the son of a Basque noble, founded the Society of Jesus in 1534. This was the most significant of regenerated and new religious orders, whose purpose was not so much to counter Protestant Reform but to refresh and enhance the Church's mission. In addition to the vows of religion, the Jesuits promised to serve the Pope in whatever capacity he identified. They were to make an outstanding contribution to Catholic reform, and to the Council of Trent through their eminent theologians like St Peter Canisius and St Robert Bellarmine. They came to England in 1542 and those of the Elizabethan age like Edmund Campion, Ralph Sherwin, and Robert Southwell inspired hard-pressed Catholics by their learning, humanism, resourcefulness in preserving the availability of the Mass in England, Wales and Scotland, and their ultimate sacrifice as martyrs.

Jesuits

By the time Ignatius died in 1556, there were a thousand Jesuits in nine European provinces, and the pioneering work of members like St Francis Xavier had opened missions in Africa, India, China, Japan, Canada and South America. By 1640, they were running five hundred influential schools, several seminaries and universities, all the while encouraging Church revival, even in the face of opposition from bishops and fellow clergy attached to their own comfort in the status quo and their monopoly of learning. Importantly, the Society inspired the founding of other orders devoted to ministering to the people, preaching the Gospel, education, and integrating prayer with action. Ignatius' major written work, the '*Spiritual Exercises*', is a pattern of contemplation, meditations, prayer, instructions and examination of conscience, highly prized by Charles Borromeo, and which has been used not only to train Jesuits but Christians of all denominations.

Philip Neri

St Philip Neri, 1515-1595, Italian priest, confessor, and Charles' friend and collaborator was renowned for his life of prayer and generosity. He founded the Congregation of the Oratory to promote the holiness of priestly life and foster good preaching. It was so called because he and his first five priest-disciples used an oratory above the

Roman church of St Girolamo to which they would call the faithful by ringing a bell. The priests lived in community and were obedient to Philip but not bound by religious vows nor asked to renounce their property. After the Pope approved the Congregation in 1575, numbers grew beyond all expectation, not least because of Philip's personality and benevolent guidance. In his home at St Girolamo, he received Cardinals, visitors from other countries, and an unending stream of the poor and the troubled. He was regarded by contemporaries as a living saint and hailed as the "Apostle of Rome."

THE COUNCIL OF TRENT

Martin Luther, John Calvin, and Ulrich Zwingli, Catholics who became leaders of the Protestant Reformation, were initially disturbed by clerical cynicism, corruption, and the abuse of indulgences. They went on to challenge Church teaching on the Mass, papal authority, the number and efficacy of the Sacraments, and the fruitful expression of Faith in good works. Calvin added that God, as absolute sovereign, determines everything that happens in human salvation, that the Fall deprived humanity of free will, and that the individual is predestined to be either damned or saved. Such reformers were unanimous in their opposition to the Mass as a Sacrifice and the presence of Christ in the Blessed Sacrament. Maybe this evolved from a rejection of the central tenet of the Catholicism which they had abandoned, their belief that the Sacrifice of Calvary needed no repetition, their disappointment with the ministerial priesthood, or the thought that the Eucharist as a celebratory meal was more attractive than the re-presentation of Christ's sacrifice on Calvary.

Pope and Emperor call a Council

Alessandro Farnese, 1468-1549, had not been totally innocent of the moral laxity and nepotism which characterised Renaissance Rome, but when he became Pope Paul III in 1534, he embarked on church renewal, appointed reforming cardinals, encouraged the energising religious orders like the Jesuits, and established the Church tribunal called the Holy Office to deal with heresy. In 1538, he excommunicated Henry VIII and placed England under interdict. Charles V, Holy Roman Emperor (of Germany, Italy, the Low countries, Spain and its colonies) pressed him to call a general council and, after two attempts thwarted by curial and political opposition, he convened the Council in the northern Italian town of Trent in 1545. He thought that all he had to do was make a routine defence of the Church, condemn the teachings of Luther and the other protesters, and it would be over in a couple of months. In fact, it took him two years to introduce even some incomplete reforms and, after transferring the Council to Bologna in 1548, he lost the Emperor's support and had to suspend it. Just as in the earlier reigns of Charlemagne and Pepin, Church government still needed the active co-operation of temporal rulers.

Pope Paul's successor, Julius III, was more interested in personal splendour. He promoted members of his family and gave the cardinal's hat to a nephew of doubtful character who was later imprisoned for murder. He reconvened the Council in 1551, but suspended it again after a year because he could not bring himself to make decisions in the face of political and military problems. He did, however, support the work of the Jesuits and welcomed England's temporary return to Catholicism during the reign of Mary Tudor. The pontificate of his successor, Marcellus II began promisingly with a restrained and inexpensive coronation. He quickly reduced the size of the Curia, discouraged nepotism by expelling his own relatives from Rome, and was just about to publish a comprehensive programme of reform when he suddenly died of a stroke only twenty-one days after assuming office.

Pope Paul IV, by nature autocratic and uncompromising, refused to reconvene the Council because he thought he could manage reform himself. He continued the revision of the Curia, not unreasonably asked bishops to reside in their dioceses and monks in their monasteries, supported the Holy Office and issued the first Index of Books which Catholics were forbidden to read. Unfortunately, he wrongly suspected Cardinals Giovanni Morone and Reginald Pole of being Lutherans, imprisoned the former and unsuccessfully demanded the latter's deportation from England to stand trial. He imposed severe restrictions on the Roman Jews whom he thought were helping Italian Protestants, confined them to a ghetto, and taxed them heavily. He roused such resentment that his death was greeted with delight by the Roman crowds who stormed the Holy Office and pulled down his statue. This was in the summer of 1559, a few weeks after Charles Borromeo had celebrated the award of his Doctorate.

Cardinal-Archbishop at twenty-two

The Conclave to find Paul's successor began on September 29th but reached no conclusion until December 26th when Charles' uncle, Govanni Medici was elected Pope and chose the name Pius IV. A few days after his coronation on January 6th 1560, he called his nephew to Rome and created him Cardinal-Deacon and Secretary of the the Papal States. Charles did not want any celebrations in Milan, preferring to have ten Masses of the Holy Spirit celebrated in Arona.

On February 8th the Pope named him administrator of the archdiocese of Milan, a huge province embracing the Venetian territories and Swiss Alps, with fifteen suffragan bishops subject to his jurisdiction, and appointed him Archpriest of Santa Maria Maggiore, Grand Penitentiary, legate of Bologna, Romagna and Ancona, Protector of Portugal, the Low Countries and the Catholic cantons of Switzerland, supervisor of the Franciscan and Carmelite Orders, the Order of the Umiliati (the Brothers of Humility), and the Knights of Malta. A sizeable income came with these appointments and cynics observed that he was just one more beneficiary of nepotism, but they were soon to change their minds as they saw that the Pope's confidence was not misplaced. Throughout his life, Charles used possessions to help the poor and support institutions essential to the health of the Church, so it was truly said that "he descended from riches to become the poorest of the poor in his diocese." He displayed energy, skill, diligence, and diplomacy in undertaking every responsibility and, even allowing for the the accelerated maturity in an age with shorter life-expectancy, the completion of an astonishing work-load indicated extraordinary gifts in a twenty-two year old.

Charles' early homes in Rome were the Vatican and then the Palazzo Colonna. His responsibilities as Secretary of State and head of his family did not prevent his continued studies, his love of music, nor the occasional hunt to keep himself in shape. His Renaissance interest in the advancement of learning prompted him to open a Literary Academy for clergy and laity who met every evening, and their discussions are recorded among his works as "Vatican Nights" which reveal that, though he was not a great classical scholar, he was more than able to hold his own in the exchanges. It was usual for such a powerful Prince of the Church to live in splendid state, but pomp and circumstance meant nothing to him, and he remained modest, humble in spirit and unmoved by the temptations of the city. During his time there he founded a charity for giving marriage dowries to penniless girls who might otherwise have finished up on the streets, organised a type of state pawn-brokers called the *Mons Pietatis* to keep the poor from being exploited by usurers, and remodelled the Baths of Diocletian, once a haunt for a variety of criminals, as a monastery for the Carthusians.

Council of Trent reconvened

Pope Pius dramatically distanced himself from his predecessor by executing two of Paul's nephews, one a cardinal and the other a duke, for political crimes. Having made his point, he felt he could pursue a more moderate course and, decided to reconvene the Council in 1562 to conclude the work of codifying Church doctrine and put an end to abuses through genuine reform. This required delicate, political negotiation especially with the European rulers, and it fell to Charles to remove obstacles and re-assemble the Council with patience, devotion, and sensitive diplomacy.

The volume of his correspondence with the legates reveals the many questions threatening to break up the Council which he had to resolve. These included the crucial matters of episcopal jurisdiction, the education of seminarists, and the discipline of the clergy which would generate strong feeling and opposition from vested interests. Then imperial demands and national interests like those advanced by the Cardinal-Archbishop of Reims on behalf of France, needed constant attention and tact and, thanks to him, two hundred and fifty-five Council Fathers assembled for the twenty-fifth and final session on December 3rd, 1563.

The Council refuted heresy, defined original sin, decreed that marriage could not be dissolved, put an end to unjust taxation and the sale of indulgences, condemned concubinage among the clergy, and brought the hierarchy of bishops under control. As well as undertaking moral reform, it defined and clarified central beliefs which had been attacked by the Protestant Reformers, and which have remained characteristic of Catholic expression:

> The freedom of the human will which has not been destroyed by original sin.
> The importance of human effort in salvation.
> The relationship between Faith and good works.
> Devotion to the Eucharist as the centre of Catholic life.
> The sacrificial character of the Mass.
> The seven sacraments and their efficacy.
> The role of the ministerial priesthood.
> The place of tradition alongside scripture.
> Devotion to Mary the Mother of God and the veneration of the saints.
> The existence of Purgatory.
> The validity of indulgences.
> The authority of Pope and Bishops.

Increased responsibilities

At a consistory held on January 26th 1564, the Pope confirmed the Council's decrees and the papal right of interpretation, and promulgated his revised *Index of Forbidden Books*. Charles was appointed to lead seven other Cardinals in supervising their implementation and, if that were not enough, he was given responsibility for the Commission for the reform of Church Music, the revision of the *Missal* and *Breviary*, and the compilation of the Roman Catechism based on the "Profession of Tridentine Faith" published to counter doctrinal abuses and ensure the availability of the deposit of Faith to everyone. (cf. *'Catechism of the Catholic Church'*, 1992). It is a measure of his achievement that Trent's resultant spiritual and institutional reform led to an affirmation of Catholic theology and related practice which would nourish the Church for four centuries. Then the Second Vatican Council, "Following in the footsteps of the Council of Trent" would "set forth authentic teaching about divine revelation and how it is handed on."

Priest and Bishop

In November 1562, while the Council was still in session, Charles' brother, Count Frederick, died unexpectedly, and he became head of the family and responsible for a great estate. Since he was still only in minor orders, his relatives begged him to renounce the clerical state in order to marry and produce heirs, a proposal which even Pope Pius supported. Charles himself was more of the opinion that his brother's early death was a sign of the fleeting nature of time, and that he should abandon the world to give himself more fully to the spiritual life and the eternal truths in the monastic state.

Pressing need for reform and renewal

In the meantime, demands for the implementation of the Council's directives were widespread, and the crowned heads of Europe were particularly insistent that if there was to be renewal, then reform should begin at the top. In the spring of 1563 the Arcbishop of Braga and Portuguese delegate, the Venerable Don Bartholomew of the Martyrs, visited Rome from Trent and did not mince words when talking to the Pope about the Curia, telling him that, "These most illustrious eminences certainly need a most illustrious reform." When they met again shortly afterwards, the Holy Father presented his nephew and joked, "You can begin your reform with this young man." Bartholomew replied, "If all the Princes of the Church were like Charles Borromeo, I should have proposed them as models of reform instead of their needing it."

Charles's dilemma

The normally reserved Charles trusted the wise and holy bishop immediately. He took him into his confidence and asked him if he thought God was really calling him to the contemplative life, or if this was a personal whim. "You know what it must be like," he confided, "to be the nephew of a Pope, and a beloved nephew at that, and you are aware of what it is to live at the court of Rome. The dangers are infinite. What ought I to do, young as I am, and without experience? God has given me an ardour for penance, and an earnest desire to prefer Him to all things; and I have some thought of entering a monastery to live as if there were only God and myself in the world." There was silence as Bartholomew prayed to the Holy Spirit for the right response, and then said, "Do not ask which is the safest way, but what is the will of God. You will do harm to the Church if you desert your post. If you loved the world, I would say flee from it. But you do not love it. God has called you to reform the Church. Finish the work you have begun." Charles said he was worried about the deplorable state of the archdiocese of Milan, and thought that he should make it his first responsibility. Bartholomew reassured him, "Take your time, take your time. Remember the Pope's age and his need of your help and presence here."

Ordained priest

Bartholomew had recognised Charles' ability and vocation to renew the human character of the Church for the benefit of God's People. Fortunately, his advice was taken and he would be proved right. Charles' dilemma was resolved, he handed family leadership to his uncle Julius, and was ordained priest in St Mary Major on September 4th, 1563. On the Feast of St Ambrose, December 7th, he was consecrated bishop in the Sistine Chapel, received the pallium, and was elevated in rank to Cardinal-Priest. His cardinalate church was that of St Praxedes, the Roman virgin of the late first century who was buried on the site with her sister St Pudentiana, both daughters of the Roman senator Pudens who is said to have been converted to Christianity by St Peter himself.

Rome

Charles virtually rebuilt the church and added a cloister and house for the monks who served there, and later he would stay here whenever he was in Rome. The church housed the Column at which Our Lord was scourged, and he would spend long hours in prayer before this relic of the Passion. Every day before his own frugal meal, he would stand at the church door distributing alms and food to the poor who flocked from the neighbouring slums. He also restored the titular churches of St Vitus and Modestus, and St Martina, which had been his when Cardinal-Deacon, and many others. All this was conducted at his own expense, as was the generous financial support which accompanied the advice he gave to the Theatines, the Jesuits and the Oratory of Philip Neri, his life-long friend in Rome.

Milan

The dreadful situation which faced the new Archbishop of Milan is a measure of his staggering achievements. Throughout the province, there were problems generated by the decay of mediaeval society and a revived interest in pagan antiquity. The Eucharist was neglected, attendance at Mass was spasmodic, many clergy led immoral, idle, and greedy lives, or were so ignorant that they could not even give Absolution in Latin. Empty churches were used as barns, and the monastic rule so ignored that monasteries were venues for balls and banquets. He had to put a stop to these junketings, and order nuns to bar their windows against the entry of the ardent young men to whom they were giving welcome. Twenty convents had to be suppressed, and even some which were allowed to remain open rebelled against change, including two led by the Pope's sisters.

Diocesan visitations

The pastoral care remembered in the Collect for his Feast explains his choice not only of seminary rectors who nurtured priests, but also of the most suitable vicars-general who represented him throughout the diocese. The first of these was Monsignor Nicolo Ormaneto who had been in the household of the English Cardinal Reginald Pole, and assistant to the Bishop of Verona. He arrived in Milan on July 1st 1564 and, at Charles' request, immediately called twelve hundred priests to a diocesan synod in order to promulgate the decrees of the Council, the first of which was clergy reform. He followed this up with a diocesan visitation to see if any notice had been taken.

In September, with no let up in pace, Charles procured the help of thirty Jesuits to help him, three of whom he appointed to the seminary which he opened two months later in November! He personally pursued ecclesiastic discipline down to the last detail, and wrote many letters on the subjects of preaching, the repression of avaricious clergy, the importance of the liturgical ceremonies with appropriate music, and the observance of the Rule in monasteries and convents. For the well-being of the individual, society and the Church, he counted the education of the young as a major pastoral responsibility, and accordingly opened schools and colleges suitably staffed.

It was no surprise that, though he was receiving every possible support from his Archbishop, Monsignor Ormaneto was beginning to feel the strain and wanted to return to his own diocese. Charles successfully appealed to Pius to let him go to Milan to restore his Vicar's confidence and tend his flock. With Pius' consent, he assembled a provincial council on October 15th 1565 and announced that if reform were to have any impact, a start must be made with his fellow prelates themselves. "We ought to walk in front and our spiritual subjects will follow more easily," he told them. The energy with which he fulfilled all that was required of himself amazed his brethren and was largely responsible for the positive report he was able to send to the Pope on November 3rd.

A new Pope

On November 6th, he went to Trent as the Pope's Legate to meet the Archduchesses Giovanna and Barbara to discuss the implications of their forthcoming marriages to the Prince of Florence and the Duke of Ferrara. Soon after he arrived, news was brought that Pope Pius was seriously ill, so he hurried back to Rome to find that his condition was incurable. He helped his beloved uncle think of his heavenly home and, with Philip Neri, comforted him until he died on December 10th 1565. Charles' holiness and administrative acumen were now so manifest and admired that when the Cardinals gathered in

Rome for Conclave, his name was on every one's lips as the next pope. He stifled such speculation, proceeded to exercise masterly diplomacy in moderating the inevitable factions, and guided the Cardinals to elect Michele Ghislieri on January 7th 1566. This was the saintly, sometimes fiery, Dominican bishop of Mondovi renowned for his remarkable kindness to the poor and the sick who, at Charles' request, took the name Pius V.

Back to Rome

He too was quick to appreciate the worth of so respected a prelate, and wanted to keep him in Rome. Charles was allowed to return to Milan for the summer, and on his way back, he made a detour to the Shrine of Our Lady of Loreto where he prayed earnestly to the Mother of God for her continued help. Back in Rome, he demonstrated how the Church with the help of the Holy Spirit renews itself from within. He continued the implementation of the Council's decisions, lifted Rome's moral tone by removing unsuitable postholders from the curia, and legislated against anti-social behaviour, bull-fighting, and prostitution. He completed the revision of the Divine Office, the Roman Missal, and the Catechism which he arranged to have translated into other major languages. More seminaries were opened, the clergy were exhorted to lead moral lives, and parish-priests obliged to instruct children for whom he established the Confraternity of Christian Doctrine. This caring and systematic instruction of the young became known as the Sunday School and, there is a testimony to Charles' work in this regard in an inscription beneath a statue in the Essex Unitarian Church of London.

Personal mortification

Charles continued to give his possessions to the poor and insisted on strict economy in matters relating to himself. He did, however, demand appropriate respect for the office and function of Cardinal-Archbishop, though his personal mortification and fasting remained so fierce that friends had to persuade him to eat a little more. Once he said that "the best way not to find the bed too cold is to go to bed colder than the bed is." There were no warming pans for him! The rules for the management of Archbishop's Palace in spiritual and temporal matters, and the care he took of its members, resulted in twenty of his circle becoming distinguished bishops or prelates who attributed their progress to the shining example they had received while in his household. One of these was the Welshman Owen Lewis, a Fellow of New College Oxford who taught at Douai and Oxford, and became Archdeacon of Cambrai. When he was sent to Rome on legal business, he made such a good impression that the Pope kept him there to handle matters relating to England. Charles ever "a robber of good men", as Philip Neri would put it, in due course would appoint him Milan's Vicar-General, and, later, Bishop of Cassano in Calabria.

Continued pastoral visitations

The detailed reports and conferences which supported Charles' administration were of a quality which made his tireless visitations all the more effective. He organised the Cathedral Canons to undertake specific theological work, like ensuring correct attitudes towards the Sacraments, and reminded them that, "he who desires to make any progress in the service of God must begin every day of his life with new ardour, must keep himself in the presence of God as much as possible, and must have no other view or end in all his actions but the divine honour." Pastoral visitations continued all the while, generating foundations on behalf of the poor, looking for the wandering sheep who were always close to his heart, and treating prisoners humanely, so much so that his court became known as "the holy tribunal."

In October 1567, he began a series of visits to the three Swiss valleys of Levantina, Bregno, and La Riviera, and found that there was much to be done. Many priests were behaving disgracefully with the result that the people in their care followed their negligent example. He faced the rigours of the visit with fortitude, travelling over difficult, sometimes dangerous terrain on horseback or on foot, often meeting violent opposition, but usually winning over both clergy and laity whom he refreshed with a new spirit.

DANGEROUS TIMES

European rulers and Spanish governors who, for personal or national reasons, wanted to overthrow or curtail the authority of the Church, resented Charles' firm independence. A case in point related to the collegiate church of Santa Maria della Scala which had been exempted from the jurisdiction of the Arcbishop of Milan by Pope Clement VII in 1531. The chapter of Canons insisted on their autonomy and refused to accept a visit from the Archbishop. Charles was left with no alternative but to impose sentence of excommunication, but as he approached the church with the document, the Canons' supporters opened fire, and he had to retreat. When the provincial Governor, the Duke of Albuquerque, made things worse by siding with the rebels, the Pope was furious and wanted to deal with the matter himself. Charles said he would handle the situation in his own way and, as it turned out, another incident would bring the Canons to a more obedient frame of mind.

Assasination attempt

The Umiliati, one of the congregations which had been placed in Charles' care, had started in the twelfth century as a lay movement, a type of Benedictine Third Order to promote poverty as a way of life in imitation of Christ and to serve the poor. However, by the sixteenth century, it had made huge profits from the wool trade and the members were living in such luxury that they had lost sight of their purpose. With tactful perseverance, Charles managed to introduce some much needed reforms but, in 1567, some who wanted a return to the former comfortable ways plotted his death. On October 26th, while he was at Evening Prayer with his household, a member in secular disguise called Farina shot Charles' in the back as he knelt at the altar. As soon as he felt the impact, he assumed he was mortally wounded, commended himself to God, and calmly requested that the Prayer should be concluded. By a miracle, the bullet fell on the floor without penetrating his clothing, though it had broken the skin and raised a slight swelling which stayed with him for the rest of his life. He made every effort to prevent the prosecution of these fellow clergy, but the civil authorities arrested the conspirators and put them to death. It was this attempt on his life which finally moved the canons of Santa Maria della Scala to ask their Archbishop's pardon, and he absolved them publically at the door of his Cathedral. Pope Pius eventually suppressed the Order of the Umiliati.

Undaunted, Charles set off on another visit to the three Swiss valleys of his diocese which also which gave him an opportunity to call on his half-sister Ortensia, a daughter his father's later marriage and now the Countesse d'Altemps. Never doubting the certainty of his cause, and with confidence in God unshaken, he went to all the Catholic cantons to stem the abuses and irregularities of doctrine on the part of both clergy and laity, and restore observance of the Rule in monasteries and convents. When he returned to Milan, he recruited experienced and dedicated missioners to go to those areas where he had discovered Protestant heresy such as that preached by Zwingli, to correct it, and bring back to the Faith those who had embraced it.

Famine and war

In 1571, the harvest failed and the whole province was struck by a terrible famine. Charles worked tirelessly, feeding as many as three thousand men, women and children a day at his own expense and inspiring others to help, including the Duke of Alberquerque who proved generous in giving alms. He fell ill himself during August but recovered quickly enough to embark on another visitation during which news was brought that the Governor was seriously ill. He returned to Milan, but only in time for the Governor's funeral and to comfort his Duchess. Two months later, there was a happier moment when the combined forces of the Papal States, Venice and Spain defeated the Turks at the battle of Lepanto in the Mediterranean. Charles was especially thankful because the Papal fleet was commanded by the father-in-law of his sister Anna. Pius V, already zealous in fostering devotion to the Rosary which he called a "compendium of the entire Gospel", instituted the Feast of Our Lady of the Rosary to be celebrated annually on October 7th in thanksgiving for the liberation of Christians from the forces of Islam.

Poor health

In 1572, Charles' health became uncertain and tuberculosis was suspected, but this did not stop him organising another diocesan synod for April. On May 1st, as the prelates were dispersing, it was announced that Pope Pius V had died. Charles was so unwell that he had not been able to say Mass for some time, and his doctors and clergy pleaded with him not to go to Rome for the Conclave. With a smile, he quoted Isaiah, "Any work founded on an individual is doomed to destruction, for it is no better then the broken staff or reed, upon which if a man lean, it will pierce his hand." Riding a horse was out of the question, so a nightmarish journey was undertaken with attendants carrying him by litter. The weather was so dreadful that one unfortunate mule fell into a raging river taking with him a packload of pills and drugs. Charles thought this a good omen, "and a sign that there is no further need of medicines."

Another conclave

After the Mass of the Holy Spirit on May 12th, the Conclave began and within twenty-four hours the Cardinal of San Sisto, Ugo Boncompagni, was elected and had taken the name Gregory XIII. Charles began to feel better, and was overjoyed that he was able to celebrate daily Mass again. Though much younger than the new Pope, he helped him frame policies to continue the Catholic Counter-Reformation in Poland, Germany and the Low Countries, implement the decisions of the Council of Trent, and support the reforming efforts by St Philip Neri, the Jesuits, and Capuchins. He sought help for himself from the Mother of God and, on his way back to Milan, again visited her shrine at Loreto.

Upon prayerful reflection, he thought it prudent to resign as Grand Penitentiary and Arch-Priest of St Mary Major, and concentrate on the next provincial council scheduled for April 1573. The headings of his preparatory notes are interesting:

"Profession of Faith and care of it.
Administration of the Sacraments.
Public Worship.
The Clergy's manner of life.
Discipline of Religious Houses and Orders."

All these points are expanded with subsidiary details, and he notes that bishops and priests are called "not to comfort and luxury but to cares and labours," and that episcopal meals are to be "frugal and temperate," but with "indulgence to the stomachs of guests"! For three weeks before diocesan synods, clergy and laity sought spiritual renewal under his direction in prayer, by frequenting the Sacraments, and hearing homilies based on the Exercises of St Ignatius.

The diocesan synod of 1574 ended in December, just in time for him to make a penitential pilgrimage to Rome for the beginning of the Holy Year. The Carthusians of Santa Maria degli Angeli invited him to celebrate Christmas with them, and persuaded him to share their modest festive meal by having a morsel of roast meat. He edified Rome by walking barefoot in procession from one Station church to another, and ascending the Scala Sancta every day on his knees, though on one occasion this nearly proved the end for one corpulent Cardinal who rashly wanted to accompany him. Perhaps it was no coincidence that he then helped the Pope renew the decree that coaches for Cardinals were not allowed.

Another incident occurred which throws light on the distribution of power between Church and State and the ensuing tensions. When the new Governor Don Luigi de Requesens assumed office, he was persuaded by some of Charles' enemies to publish letters which falsely accused him of flouting royal authority and claiming unjustified rights for the Church. At first Charles maintained a dignified silence, but when he was subjected to further libels he reluctantly excommunicated the Grand-Chancellor and, by implication, the Governor who retaliated by placing restrictions on the meetings of confraternities and confiscating the Castle of Arona. There were rumours of even more sinister plots, but Charles remained tranquil and continued to work with characteristic energy, even though the Governor had placed an armed watch on Archbishop's Palace. Gregory XIII would not tolerate this and compelled the Governor to make satisfaction to his Cardinal-Archbishop. When he did so, Charles absolved him from all the penalties and censures which otherwise would have been imposed.

Milan hit by plague

In 1576, he was at Lodi presiding at the funeral of the Bishop when he heard that the plague which had already affected Venice and Mantua had now reached Milan, a situation soon aggravated by a food shortage resulting from the impact on commerce and agriculture. With no concern for himself he returned at once, brought his will up to date, prepared for death, and gave himself entirely to his people. He defied contagion unhesitatingly as he visited those in plague-stricken houses, comforted the badly infected in St Gregory's Hospital, and took the Last

Sacraments to the dying, all of whom were touched by the warmth and kindness of one who could appear severe. He managed to persuade some of the clergy to help him and then, in a plea for God's mercy on the suffering, did public penance, walking barefoot through the city with a rope around his neck and carrying a huge Crucifix.

When the plague abated early in 1577, Charles wrote the '*Memoriale*' for his suffragan bishops pointing out the lessons to be learned from its visitation. "Deliverance from pestilence," he said, "was not by our prudence which was caught asleep, not by science or the doctors who could not discover the sources of contagion much less a cure, not by the care of those in authority who abandoned the city, but only by the mercy of God." Not long afterwards, the Bishop of Famagosta completed a visitation of the Milan diocese which the plague had interrupted. He announced from the altar steps of the Cathedral the results of his inspection and said that he had found perfection in discipline and order and "what is not perfect will soon become so." It was a far cry from the state of neglect and immorality which had greeted the Archbishop when he first took up residence, and testifies to what had been accomplished in the space of a decade through arduous and incessant work. Charles was the first to attribute progress to God, and was always confident that His help would be forthcoming.

A Tireless Reformer

Friendship with Philip Neri

When all traces of the plague had finally disappeared in January 1578, Charles held a diocesan synod, and persuaded the Canons of his Cathedral to live together with him in Archbishop's Palace. His close friendship with Philip Neri had helped him appreciate the strength which the Fathers of the Oratory derived from their community life which enhanced personal activity. He told them that they were blessed to be living under the guidance of so great a master, though when he tried to recruit some of them, Philip teased him with being "a daring robber of good souls" and "a rogue who would strip one altar to adorn another." Whenever the Cardinal-Archbishop visited the room of the simple priest, he would kneel and kiss his hand and then, on their knees, they would recite the Divine Office together. He said that he always found Philip "a man of marvellous sincerity and singular holiness," two shared qualities which cemented their friendship. He asked him to found a branch of the Oratory in Milan, but Philip thought the time was not yet ripe. He did, however, say that he would send two volunteers to Milan the following year, but for some reason they were side-tracked and never arrived, much to Charles' disappointment.

Founding the Oblates

He also appreciated the great help other religious orders had given him, especially the Jesuits distinguished by the presence of St Francis Borgia, the Theatines by that of St Andrew Avelino, and the Barnabites of St Anthony Zaccaria who supported him whole-heartedly by their missionary activities and dedication to the education of clergy and laity. He concluded that he, too, needed a body of priests in sympathy with his spirit and ideals to live in community and support one another to the best possible advantage in the care of souls.

He therefore decided to found a congregation of secular clergy under the patronage of Our Lady and St Ambrose with the title of 'Oblates of St Ambrose', later 'of St Charles'. He took the first draft of the Rule for his Oblates to Philip Neri for his opinion, and was advised not to include the vow of poverty. Charles demurred, so Philip suggested they consult a Capuchin lay brother called Felix for his judgement. Brother *'Deo Gratias'*, as he was nicknamed, immediately put his finger on the article dealing with the vow of poverty and said, "This should be omitted." Charles recognised that this and other suggestions he made were undoubtedly wise, and adopted them without hesitation. The humble friar is now remembered as St Felix of Cantalicio.

Charles was the Superior of the Congregation and was delighted to be with his brethren who looked to him as a father and undertook the tasks and responsibilities he identified in parishes, schools, seminaries and confraternities. The work-load was heavy, but he led them never to lose sight of the essential balance between the time given to God in prayer and the activities of their calling.

A further visit was made to the Swiss valleys, the Ursuline Nuns were established at Anta Sofia, and he had a protracted correspondence with Cardinal Enriquez who had succeeded to the throne of Portugal after King Sebastian had died in battle against the Moors. The frail and elderly prelate kept writing to Charles about obtaining a dispensation from his vows in order to marry and have heirs. He finally received a blunt reply to the effect that such an idea had no precedent and, in any case, at his age marriage would probably be the death of him! The sense of humour had not disappeared.

Pilgrimage

In thanksgiving for deliverance from the plague, Charles had vowed that he would make a pilgrimage to the Holy Shroud which was at Chambery after its transportation from Cyprus to keep it safe from the Turks. Shortly after the victory of Lepanto, he set off with twelve companions including his confessor Father Adorno. He intended to walk all the way but when the Duke of Savoy heard this, he had the Shroud brought to Turin Cathedral where it has remained ever since. Even so it was still a trek of ninety miles in autumnal weather. The soles of his feet had such blisters that the barber was called to lance them. One of the clumsy cuts he made took a long time to heal, but nothing stopped this "soul without a body" from walking the streets of Turin to meet the people, and the Cathedral could not accommodate the numbers who came to Mass when he was celebrating. On his way home, he went to the Holy Mountain of Varallo between Monte Rosa and Lake Maggiore, a shrine with a Franciscan church and thirty-eight chapels dedicated to the Passion. In the bitter cold he meditated on the mysteries of the Passion, snatching only a couple of hours' sleep and breaking a twenty-four hour's fast with on a little bread and water after he had said Mass. As well as in thanksgiving for the end of the plague, these penances were a preparation for a further storm which was brewing on the horizon.

Jealousies and rivalry

The Spanish and Milanese nobles and Senators had fled Milan as soon as the plague arrived to return only when it was safe to indulge in the amusements the city offered. Charles' fervent faith and selfless concern for others reproached their own tepidity and, during the winter, 1578-9, they stirred up trouble. They maliciously interpreted his alms-giving to the poor, his personal visits to the sick and the dying, and his making provision for orphans, widows and the destitute, as a treacherous plot to gain popularity and win supreme authority for himself to the disadvantage of the emperor Philip II.

The Marquis of Ayamonte who was now Governor, questioned ecclesiastic jurisdiction and, contrary to the Cardinal-Archbishop's instructions, ordered the annual carnival to be celebrated on the first Sunday of Lent rather than on Shrove Tuesday. He also supported a Sicilian Jesuit, Mazzarino, described as having "less sense than years", who denounced "ecclesiastic usurpers" and clerics who "advertised themselves by going barefoot and wearing sackcloth." Charles' charity could overlook and pardon personal insults but he could not allow episcopal dignity and the rights of the Church to be attacked. Mazzarino was forbidden to preach and summoned to Rome by the Father General of the Jesuits to be tried for heresy. He was acquitted but the ban on preaching was not lifted until Charles himself made a plea to Rome on his behalf.

Ayamonte's next ploy was to complain to the Pope about Charles' behaviour, his banning of public sports on Sundays and Feasts, increasing the number of abstinence days in Lent, and erecting barriers in churches so that men and women could not see each other! Charles went to Rome for Gregory XIII's judgement.The Pope who admired what had been accomplished in the province and especially the Swiss valleys, confirmed Charles' authority and sent an appropriate message back to Milan which the envoys were rightly embarrassed to deliver.

As ever, the Cardinal-Archbishop had shown a fearless and indomitable spirit, but an earlier letter shows that he was not immune to heartache. "I am sure that hopes founded on men are to be dreaded, the most deceitful and the fastest to vanish. But when action is based on justice, and for the glory of God, he gives His protection and help, so that an enterprise, though deprived of human help and approval, is successful. God has the greatest care for those abandoned by the world, and on such occasions manifests his mercy and pity all the more." Ayamonte's animosity was born of jealousy, and his petulant comment to Charles after the plague is an inadvertent tribute. "It is painful for me to see how everyone in Milan loves you. You are almost worshipped while I, minister of the most powerful king, am barely tolerated."

Reform and unpopularity

Charles returned from Rome via Florence, Bologna, Venice, regenerating the ecclesiastical spirit, and making an extra effort in the diocese of Brescia, which he found "so lacking in Christian institutions, and the people so cold toward religion." He discovered churches ruined and deserted, altars defiled, immorality, ignorance, and a loss of Faith which gave zealous Lutheran and Calvinist missionaries great opportunities. His remedy was to re-educate the older priests when possible, and train young ones to hold their own when confronting Protestant heresy. He founded a special seminary for Swiss priests to complement the one recently opened in Milan, and the Jesuit College now at Locarno. One moment of light during the Brescia visitation was meeting Luigi Gonzaga of the Castiglione family related to the Borromeos through the network of marriages linking the great families of northern Italy. Charles gave first Holy Communion to the future St Aloysisus Gonzaga of the Society of Jesus.

Having set in motion the essential reform of religious houses and the secular clergy, he had no illusions about his unpopularity when he forwarded his findings to Rome. "I expect outcries and proposals against which I must fortify myself. The enmity shown me, above all by the clergy, is unthinkable." As he left, he took some comfort in the thought that the Convent of Poor Clares he had founded in the city was a power house of prayer from which the spirit of Christianity would permeate other religious houses, presbyteries, and homes. When he eventually arrived back in Milan, the people were greatly relieved because they had feared he might never return.

In April 1580 Charles was told that the Marquis of Ayamonte, was dying and was asking for him. He immediately suspended the Brescia visitation and rode to Milan, going straight to the Governor's room. Ayamonte was beyond speech and in obvious torment until Charles knelt beside him, calming, consoling his old adversary until he breathed his last. His temporary successor was an unobtrusive official who managed things peacefully until the appointment of the Duke of Terra Nueva, a devout and loyal son of the Church who helped altercations with former Spanish Governors to be forgotten, and gave Charles a chance to continue reform and reorganisation without added distractions.

His English visitors

In May he welcomed twelve English priests on their way from Rome to the English mission, among them Edmund Campion, Ralph Sherwin and Robert Persons. He had already met the group in Rome and, knowing that they were on their way to certain death, there was nothing he did not do to make their stay as joyous as possible. He appreciated Persons' practical ability, efficiency, and dedication to duty. Campion, on the other hand, was the eloquent, lively, imaginative classical scholar, and a contrast to Charles' more austere personality, yet, during the eight day stay, a deep friendship was forged between the two who shared an ardent charity and heroic selflessness. Sherwin who, like Campion, was a Classics Fellow of Exeter College Oxford, preached before the Cardinal-Archbishop but it was the latter who spoke on the less formal occasions and entranced Charles and his household gathered in the great hall of the palace after dinner. Persons wrote of Charles, "He had several and most learned godly talks with us, about contempt of this world and a perfect zeal for Christ's service, whereof we saw so rare example in himself and his austere and laborious life, he being nothing truly but skin and bone, through continual pains, fasting and penance. So that had he not said a word, we should have left him greatly edified and most encouraged."

Edmund Campion and Ralph Sherwin were martyred together at Tyburn eighteen months later on December 1st, 1581. The Office for Ralph Sherwin and Companions, granted to the English College in 1936, makes special mention of St Charles Borromeo in the fifth lesson. "He was charming and said that it would give him the greatest joy to offer the hospitality of his house in Milan to those defenders of so noble a Cause journeying to their country, and he was glad to express this desire in a letter sent to the Rector which today is reverently preserved in the College." The letter dated June 30th 1580 to Father Agazzari, Rector of the English College Rome, reads "I saw and willingly entertained those English who went from here the other day, as their goodness so well deserved, and the cause for which they embarked on that journey. If in future your Reverence should send others, be assured that I will take care to receive them with all charity and that it will be a great pleasure to me to have the opportunity to perform those duties of hospitality which are so fitting for a bishop towards Catholics of that nation."

"A Light to the Church"

In September 1582, Charles left his diocese in the capable hands of Monsignor Owen Lewis and made his last journey to Rome. Still pursuing the aims of the Council of Trent, he wanted ratification of the decisions taken during his recent provincial council. He stayed at the monastery attached to his church of St Praxedes, and used it as a base for the next twelve months to make pastoral visits to Siena, Mantua, the Swiss Cantons and the Grisons. He began in the Mesolcina Valley where he had to deal with heresy, witchcraft and sorcery, in Reveredo sadly discovering that the chief sorcerer was the parish-priest. In Bellinzona and Ascona he met opposition from the disobedient Bishop of Coire, and more heretics who spread false rumours that he was an agent of Spain acting against the inhabitants of the Grisons. Nevertheless, there was no stopping him and, before he returned to Milan, there were signs that his efforts to preserve the Faith were blessed by God and proving fruitful.

Onset of illness

Early in 1584, he was confined to bed for a while with a painful leg inflammation, but struggled up to hold a conference with sixty rural deans to identify and attend to the needs of the diocese. Among the matters which concerned him was the absence of proper care for the sick once they had been discharged from hospital, so he initiated the foundation of convalescent homes. During September and October he visited Vercelli, Monte Varallo, made another pilgrimage to the Holy Shroud in Turin, and in this opportunity to contemplate Our Lord's death and burial, calmly prepared for his own. With the help of his confessor, Father Adorno, he made a General Confession according to the Ignatian Spiritual Exercises.

On October 24th he was feverish but able to say Mass and distribute Holy Communion. Certain that time was running out, he dealt with the usual, voluminous correspondence, and worked even harder if that were possible. He was particularly anxious that the college he had designed for Ascona should be completed as soon as possible and, in view of his state of health, undertook yet one more incredible journey. On October 29th, he rode to Arona, crossed by boat to Canobbio, and continued overland to Asconia. He satisfied himself that all was well with the college and returned to spend the night in Canobbio, feeling very weak, though the fever had decreased. In the morning he was ferried back to Arona and stayed with the Jesuits in their novitiate which he had founded. On November 1st, happily the Feast of All Saints, he celebrated what was to be his last Mass with them and gave Communion to the novices and the many faithful who attended.

Death at forty-six

The next day was All Souls, but he could only assist at Mass and receive Communion before being escorted back to Milan by his cousin Rene. For a while there seemed to be a slight improvement but then the fever returned with a vengeance and his doctors knew the end was near. The Last Sacraments were administered, Prayers for the Dying said, and the Passion read. On November 3rd, with Father Bascape and Father Adorno at his bedside, Charles spoke his last words, "Ecce venio", Behold I come, and went to His Lord. He was forty-six years old. The servants who removed his coarse woollen clothes found his back scarred from flagellation and his skin chafed by the patched hair-shirt. The doctor who performed the embalming said he found "a skeleton; nothing on the bones but skin," and that the Saint "had died like a lamp that is extinguished when all the oil has burnt out." On November 7th Cardinal Nicolo Sfondrato, Bishop of Cremona, later Pope Gregory XIV, presided over the Solemn Requiem and brother Cardinals eulogised the " Prince of Pastors", a "pattern of virtue and true nobility", and "a second Ambrose", the fourth century Doctor of the Church and illustrious predecessor as Archbishop of Milan.

Charles was immediately hailed as a saint. Most of the population of Milan filed past the cathedral chapel in which the body of their Archbishop lay in state. With their

Rosaries and Crucifixes they reached through the railings to touch the feet that had walked the streets of the city in the service of God and on their behalf. Soon every house had his picture, crowds prayed for his help as they knelt at his tomb, and the cry of "Miracle!" was heard repeatedly and with justification. As the cult widened, the anniversary Requiem was replaced by the solemn celebration of the Mass of the day, and it was obvious that canonisation would not long be delayed.

The remarkable contribution he had made to life in Europe is evident in the mass of his correspondence with Popes and emperors eager for his opinion and guidance. Of domestic interest is his admiration of St John Fisher, the Bishop of Rochester whose writings in defence of Church tradition had made a decisive contribution to the Council of Trent, and whose picture he had always carried with him. The honour English Catholics paid Charles was stimulated by the swift circulation of biographical details, and personal information supplied by his friend St Edmund Campion of the Society of Jesus.

In 1595 Charles' cousin, Cardinal Federigo Borromeo, was appointed Archbishop of Milan and proved a worthy successor. His virtue and zeal had flourished under the guidance of his cousin and St Philip Neri and, in a fruitful ecclesiastic career, he continued their promotion of intellectual culture and social refinement founded on a practical religious life. He founded the Ambrosian Library which, after the Bodleian in Oxford, was the first genuine public library in Europe. When he addressed the twenty-first Synod of Milan, he immortalised the memory of his cousin's tireless visitations to the people of his far-reaching diocese. "Glorious mountains, blessed valleys, hallowed paths, which still bear traces of the work of Charles, where with the help of Heaven, he won such glorious victories over deathless enemies. How lovely too are those dear places which once housed a fleshless body, a bodiless soul, and where poverty was enriched by the true splendours of the purple."

Journey to sainthood

In 1603, he led an embassy to Rome to ask Pope Clement VIII to consider the request for canonisation not only from Lombardy but also from Philip III of Spain, Charles Emmanuel of Savoy, Ranuzio Farnese of Parma, the Doge of Venice, the Grand Duke of Tuscany, the King of Poland, the Catholic Swiss Cantons, and all the religious orders. Clement's death and the brief papacy of Leo XI, who died within a month of election, delayed the progress of the cause, and it was not until November 1st 1610 that Pope Paul V in St Peter's Basilica raised Charles to the honours of the altar. The ceremonial panegyric stated, "He was always a giver of light which no clouds of weakness or passion could ever darken, no bodily obstacle obscure. When he left the world he was not extinguished but began an eternity in heaven, there to give light to the Church he loved so deeply." Acknowledgement was made of his utter devotion as a reforming Pastor in an important diocese at a time when it was most needed, and his conspicuous influence in the Counter-Reformation, especially in the fields of clerical reform and education, and in Religious Education through the Catechism.

In Art he has been represented in his Cardinal's robes, walking barefoot and carrying a cross. Sometimes there is a rope around his neck and a hand raised in blessing to commemorate his work and penance during the plague of 1576. A portrait by Guiseppe Crespi hangs in the Ambrosian Gallery in Milan, and in Rome's Chiesa Nuova (New Church) there is a painting by Carlo Maratta of Charles and his fellow great reformer, Ignatius of Loyola, standing beside the enthroned Blessed Virgin Mary. Sometimes the crowned *"Humilitas"* from the Borromeo coat of arms is a reminder that he used it for his own insignia. A memorial was erected to him in Milan Cathedral, as well a statue, seventy feet high, on the hill above Arona by admirers of the leader of the Catholic Counter-Reformation, and three churches in Rome are dedicated to him.

In Milan Cathedral's crypt-chapel designed by Pellegrini, the body of St Charles Borromeo lies enshrined in a silver and glass reliquary given by Philip IV of Spain. His heart, pectoral cross, and some blood-stained linen were given by Cardinal Federigo to the

Lombard church in Rome. The heart which burned with such love for God is in a heart-shaped golden reliquary aptly surrounded by flames and rays of light. When the heart is exposed, pictures are distributed to the faithful with this prayer printed: "May we be kindled with the fire of divine charity with which his heart burned."

Society of St Charles Borromeo

In 1845, Franz Xavier Dieringer, the professor of Catholic theology in the university of Bonn, founded the Society of St Charles Borromeo to encourage the diffusion of edifying, instructive, and entertaining literature, under the protection of the Hierarchy. The Saint was invoked with the prayer "O Saintly reformer, animator of spiritual renewal of priests and religious, you organised true seminaries and wrote a standard catechism. Inspire all religious teachers and authors of catechetical books. Move them to love and transmit only that which can form true followers of the Teacher who was divine. Amen."

Charles' legacy

Charles knew the importance of his work and preserved all his mandates, pastoral letters, and the conclusions of the provincial councils he called, which provided such a detailed interpretation of the Council of Trent that he has been called "Doctor of Bishops." Other items of his literary bequest include a collection of letters, discourses, and homilies. He had worked to overcome the youthful speech impediment, but listeners from every walk of life said they always forgot the orator himself when he preached because they were transported by the great truths they heard explained, and then the longest sermons seemed but a brief moment. When they were published in Milan in five volumes in 1748, they proved so popular that they were widely translated.

Practice what you preach

An extract from a sermon Charles preached at his final synod on the subject 'Practice what you preach' has a universal applicability and encapsulates the wisdom and sanctity of his life.

"We are morally weak, I admit it, but God has given us the means by which we can easily find the help we need, if we want to be helped. A priest, for example, might wish to have the integrity of life expected of him, to be chaste, and his behaviour angelic as it should be, but forgets the means he must adopt: fasting and prayer, avoiding evil company and dangerous friendships. Such a man complains that as soon as he comes to choir to sing the divine office, or prepares for Mass, a thousand distractions invade his mind, enticing it away from God. But how had he behaved in the sacristy before going into choir or beginning Mass? Did he make a real effort to compose his thoughts, and what activity did he choose to make sure that his attention did not wander?

"Shall I tell you how to go from strength to strength? Let us say you have managed for once to be attentive in choir. Now ask yourself how you are going to be more attentive next time and make your service more pleasing to God. What has happened is that the tiniest fire of divine love has been lit in you, but do not take it out into the icy blast. Keep the furnace door shut so that it does not die out. In other words, draw back from idle gossip, and those distractions which can be avoided, and keep your mind firmly on God.

"If it is your duty to preach and to teach, concentrate on what is essential to fulfilling your responsibility. Make sure that your life and conduct are sermons in themselves, and do not give others the chance to purse their lips or shake their heads during you sermons because they have heard you before, preaching one thing, and then seen you doing the exact opposite.

If your task is the care of souls, then do not neglect your own, or spend yourself so completely that you have nothing left for yourself. Of course you must look after the souls entrusted to your care but not to the extent that you forget your own. My brothers, understand that there is nothing quite so necessary to all churchmen as mental prayer which paves the way for all our actions, that accompanies them and follows them. As the Psalmist says, 'I will sing and I will understand'. When you administer the sacraments, try to understand what you are doing; when celebrating Mass, consider what you are offering; when singing in choir, remember to whom you are speaking and what you are saying to Him; and if you are in charge of souls, remember in whose blood they have been washed.

"If everything we do is done in love, we shall easily overcome the many difficulties that come our way every day we live in the world, and then we shall find the strength to bring forth Christ in ourselves and in others." (cf. *Office of Readings*, November 4th).

Supporting priests

As the peerless model of the reforming bishop, Charles was convinced that he was called to to revive the ecclesiastic spirit by guiding and supporting "the clergy whom Our Lord calls the salt of the earth, who season the world with the Christian spirit of perfect humility, meekness, patience, charity, devotion, and contempt for the world." He said it was not enough merely to know the names of virtues, for unless priests were imbued with this spirit, they could not transmit it to others. "To be disengaged from the world, and dead to themselves; to love employment in the business of our Heavenly Father, is the characteristic of the minister of the Altar. So it was with the many pastors who became saints." He maintained that as their name and office imply, the clergy are distinct from the laity, by virtue of their specific education, ministry, life, and conversation. "No matter how much a cleric is filled with the spirit of his profession, it can quickly be extinguished by too close a contact with the world, with its love of vanity, pleasure, riches, and honour. The reformation of the manners of the people depends very much on that of the clergy, and as it is with the priest, so shall it be with the people."

Vatican II and Charles Borromeo

The 'Decree on the Bishops' Pastoral Office in the Church' published by the Second Vatican Council, 1965, illustrates a continued indebtedness to his inspiration. "The Fathers confide to seminary directors and teachers the duty of forming Christ's future priests… and entreat those who are preparing for the priestly ministry to realize that the hope of the Church and the salvation of souls is entrusted to them. Priestly training should be pursued and perfected even after the seminary course of studies has been completed, and Episcopal Conferences should use the most effective procedures available, for example, pastoral institutes, conferences, and projects to introduce younger clergy to apostolic activity and to develop their priestly lives."